D1088325

JENNIFER ANISTON:

FROM FRIENDS TO FILMS

EXTRAORDINARY SUCCESS WITH A HIGH SCHOOL DIPLOMA OR LESS

JENNIFER ANISTON:

FROM FRIENDS TO FILMS

by Kim Etingoff

Mason Crest

920
Aniston

-31 3609

JENNIFER ANISTON: *FROM FRIENDS TO FILMS*

Mason Crest
370 Reed Road
Broomall, Pennsylvania 19008
www.masoncrest.com

Printed and bound in the United States of America.

First printing
9 8 7 6 5 4 3 2 1

Library of Congress Cataloging-in-Publication Data

Etingoff, Kim.
  Jennifer Aniston / by Kim Etingoff.
     p. cm. — (Extraordinary success with a high school diploma or less)
   ISBN 978-1-4222-2480-9 (hard cover) — ISBN 978-1-4222-2293-5 (series hardcover) — ISBN 978-1-4222-9353-9 (ebook)
   1. Aniston, Jennifer—Juvenile literature. 2. Actors—United States—Biography—Juvenile literature. I. Title.
  PN2287.A62E85 2012
  791.4302'8092—dc23
  [B]
                                        2011020321

Produced by Harding House Publishing Services, Inc.
www.hardinghousepages.com
Interior design by Camden Flath.
Cover design by Torque Advertising + Design.

CONTENTS

INTRODUCTION

Finding a great job without a college degree is hard to do—but it's possible. In fact, more and more, going to college doesn't necessarily guarantee you a job. In the past few years, only one in four college graduates find jobs in their field. And, according to the U.S. Bureau of Labor Statistics, eight out of the ten fastest-growing jobs don't require college degrees.

But that doesn't mean these jobs are easy to get. You'll need to be willing to work hard. And you'll also need something else. The people who build a successful career without college are all passionate about their work. They're excited about it. They're committed to getting better and better at what they do. They don't just want to make money. They want to make money doing something they truly love.

So a good place for you to start is to make a list of the things you find really interesting. What excites you? What do you love doing? Is there any way you could turn that into a job?

Now talk to people who already have jobs in that field. How did they get where they are today? Did they go to college—or did they find success through some other route? Do they know anyone else you can talk to? Talk to as many people as you can to get as many perspectives as possible.

According to the U.S. Department of Labor, two out of every three jobs require on-the-job training rather than a college degree. So your next step might be to find an entry-level position in the field that interests you. Don't expect to start at the top. Be willing to learn while you work your way up from the bottom.

That's what almost all the individuals in this series of books did: they started out somewhere that probably seemed pretty distant from their end goal—but it was actually the first step in their journey. Celebrity Simon Cowell began his career working in a mailroom. Jim Skinner, who ended up running McDonald's Corporation, started out flipping burgers. World-famous cook Rachael Ray worked at a candy counter. All these people found incredible success without a college degree—but they all had a dream of where they wanted to go in life . . . and they were willing to work hard to make their dream real.

Ask yourself: Do I have a dream? Am I willing to work hard to make it come true? The answers to those questions are important!

CHAPTER 1
A PROMISING START

Words to Know

aspiring: Someone who is aspiring is hoping to become something or achieve something.

interdisciplinary: Interdisciplinary has to do with studies that involve more than one discipline or area of study. For example, a student would be likely to read books in English class that related to what she was also learning in social studies; her math assignments might be related to her science studies; or she might do a project that required her to use math, reading, writing, history, and science to create the final product.

traditional: Something that is traditional follows older ways of doing things.

cultivate: To cultivate something means to encourage it to grow.

specialized: Something that is specialized focuses on one particular, special area.

passionate: If you are passionate about something, you are very excited about it. You are willing to devote a lot of your time and energy to it.

It's the night of the Emmy Awards, back in 2002. Hundreds of people face the stage, not to mention the millions of people watching around the world in their own homes. Most of the awards have already been given out and it's almost the end of the ceremony—but they still have to announce the winner of the category for Outstanding Lead Actress in a Comedy Series. Five famous women are nominated, and all are very talented. But only one can win, and the crowd quiets down in anticipation of the announcement. The two presenters on stage look down at their card. They pause . . . and then they read out the name of Jennifer Aniston.

Jennifer sure acts surprised when she's announced as the winner, but probably no one else is very shocked. Jennifer has starred in the hit TV show *Friends* since 1994 and has since become immensely famous. Millions of people watch *Friends* every week, and millions of people love Jennifer Aniston, who plays the part of quirky Rachel Green. She's part of what makes the show so popular.

The actress rushes up to the stage, wearing a beautiful gown. She thanks her coworkers, her family, and her friends. She says, "I just have to say thank you, from the bottom of my heart. This has been the greatest nine years of my entire life," meaning her time on *Friends*. This was definitely a high point of her career, and of her entire life.

In 2002, when Jennifer won this Emmy, she was only thirty-five. She had been nominated for other Emmys before, and she had already won many other awards for her work on *Friends*; this Emmy was just further proof of her successful career. She would go on to win many more awards.

The College Choice

Perhaps one of the most surprising things about Jennifer is that she became so successful without ever going to college. In the last

Jennifer's father is actor John Aniston, known to many for his role on the soap opera Days of Our Lives.

Jennifer was born in Los Angeles, California, the center of the acting world.

few decades, more and more people are going to college to further their education. It's hard to become a scientist, a professor, or a businessperson without getting some sort of college degree. In fact, over 70 percent of 2009 high school graduates went on to college. There's a lot of pressure to go on after high school, and a lot of people don't even think twice about applying for college.

However, college isn't always necessary to achieve success. Some people are ready to enter the workforce right after high school, because they are more mature, know what they want to do in life, and are willing to work hard.

This describes Jennifer Aniston. Even though she didn't go to college, she still valued a good education. However, she knew what she wanted to do at a young age. She was talented enough and driven enough to pursue her dreams and to accomplish what she did without attending college. Her early life proved that she had what it takes to become a successful actress.

The Really Early Years

Jennifer Joanna Aniston was born on February 11, 1969. She was born in Los Angeles, California, a good starting place for an *aspiring* actress. Los Angeles and Hollywood is filled with actors, directors, producers, and other people involved in the television and movie industries. Her family life also pointed her in the direction of acting.

Jennifer's parents are Nancy Dow and John Aniston; both were actors. Her mom Nancy briefly appeared in a few films and TV shows in the 1960s. Her Greek American father was an even more serious and well-known actor. He was most famous for his role as one of the main characters on the soap opera *Days of Our Lives*, but he also appeared in several other television shows. In addition, Jennifer's godfather is actor Telly Savalas, a famous TV and movie actor who starred in the show *Kojak*, and in several films. Jennifer was definitely surrounded by the idea of acting, from the moment she was born!

Jennifer wasn't really that focused on acting when she was little, though. Her family moved around a lot when she was a child, so Jennifer moved away from Los Angeles at an early age and ended up in New York City. Her parents divorced when she was nine, and she lived with both parents at different times.

She even lived in Greece for a year when she was five. Her father was originally from Greece, but he had moved to the United States with his parents when he was young. His last name was Anastassakis, though his family changed it to sound more American once they came to the United States. So when he returned to Greece for a while to pursue work, he brought his daughter with him for a year.

Both of her parents eventually remarried. Her dad married Sherry Rooney and had a son named Alexander, giving Jennifer a younger half-brother. Her mother also remarried and had a son, John T. Melick.

Early Education

Part of the reason why Jennifer never went to college is because she received such a good early education. She started out at the Rudolf Steiner School in New York City. The Steiner School is an example of a Waldorf school. Waldorf schools are an alterna-

Jennifer didn't go to a typical high school, but her early education helped shape the rest of her life.

tive approach to education. The theory behind Waldorf schools is very **interdisciplinary.** Students get to experience a wide range of subjects and are taught to be enthusiastic about learning. There's less emphasis on testing and on learning exactly the same thing; students learn at their own pace. All in all, there is less structure than in **traditional** schools.

Waldorf schools are also very big on the arts. Dancing, painting, acting, music, and writing are all very important. Students don't just go to art or music class for an hour every other day. They use art to learn about other things, and it is part of class lessons every day.

A Waldorf school is a perfect place for a future actress (or artist or musician) to get an education. Jennifer probably showed an early talent for art partly because she went to a school that emphasized art so strongly. She started learning to be more independent and began to *cultivate* her creativity even before she was ten years old—and when she was eleven, one of her school paintings was displayed in the New York Metropolitan Museum of Art!

She wasn't necessarily focused on acting, however, even though she was in the drama club. Jennifer didn't start her career as a child star the way some celebrities do. But she definitely had a creative mind that would serve her well later on during her acting career.

High School for Actors

When Jennifer was a little older, she enrolled in the Fiorello H. LaGuardia High School of Music & Art and Performing Arts, also called the "Fame" school. This is a public school in New York City that specializes in teaching students different kinds of art. Students still take math, history, science, and English, but they also focus on art. Some take dancing, some paint, some play music, and some perfect their acting skills. To graduate with a certificate in art, they have to spend a lot of time during their school years performing or creating in their chosen art field.

LaGuardia High School has produced several famous artists, musicians, writers, and actors. Many students take what they learned in high school and turn it into a successful entertainment or arts career. Al Pacino, Sarah Michelle Gellar, Robert de Niro, and Wesley Snipes are all examples of famous actors who started out at LaGuardia. It's no surprise that Jennifer Aniston is among their number.

This kind of education is a little different from what most kids get in high school; it's a little more like college. Students at *specialized* schools like this one often know what they're *passionate* about, and they take classes in it as early as fourteen or fifteen. After four years of dancing, painting, or acting, students have a lot of skills that others don't. They've been training for several years by the time they graduate.

Of course, plenty of students who go to these kinds of schools end up going to college too, to keep on learning in an academic setting. But by the time she graduated in 1987, Jennifer had learned enough about acting to start out on her own. She knew she wanted to act, and so she set out to do it.

CHAPTER 2
JENNIFER'S EARLY CAREER: LEADING UP TO SUCCESS

Words to Know
parodies: Parodies are spoofs that make fun of other movies or TV shows.

Even though Jennifer Aniston clearly possessed some talent at a young age, and she had a good education to start with, she still needed to work hard to get to where she is now. Before she found success, she struggled during the early years of her career. It wasn't until later that she became the big-name star she is today.

Post-Graduation

Jennifer graduated high school in 1987 and decided not to go to college. Unlike a lot of recent high school graduates these days, she wanted to start working right away, not continue her formal schooling. Her father said of her, "I don't think any father who knows anything about this business [acting] would be thrilled to have a daughter in it. I wanted her to go to college, and she just didn't want to. She was anxious to get on with it. Once she decided what she wanted to do, she was very driven."

Jennifer obviously already had one thing in place: her determination to do well in life and in acting. But even though she had graduated from a special high school, she was still young, and she didn't have any experience working outside of high school. She continued to live with her mother in New York City. But she didn't just sit at home and do nothing!

Acting was what she had studied in high school, and acting was what she had made up her mind she was going to do once she got out of school. But acting is a hard career to get into. You generally either need to know someone in the acting business, work really hard to get noticed, or have a lot of luck. Fortunately, Jennifer had all three. She was already familiar with the entertainment industry because of her family and godfather, and because of her experiences in high school. She was also determined to find good acting jobs. And eventually, she was lucky enough to make it big. At first, it was hard for the beginning actress, but she continued to live in New York City, searching for acting jobs in Manhattan's Off-Broadway theaters.

However, she also had to earn some money, so in addition to looking for acting jobs, Jennifer worked several jobs before she made it big—and she wasn't too proud to work hard at whatever job she could find. For example, she worked at a burger joint for while. Her other part-time jobs included a telemarketer, a waitress, and a bike messenger. (Coincidentally, she frequently later

Jennifer knew she wanted to act from an early age, but reaching her dreams wasn't easy. Her passion for acting and drive to succeed helped Jennifer get to where she is today.

Jennifer's early acting career wasn't perfect, but it helped her learn a lot about being a working actor.

played waitresses on TV shows and movies, including *Friends* and *Office Space*.)

Eventually, Jennifer landed roles in two Off-Broadway productions called *For Dear Life* and *Dancing on Checker's Grave*. These experiences gave her more exposure to acting. But Off-Broadway shows weren't enough for her, and she kept looking for work outside of the theater. She wanted to star on television, and she soon made the move to find TV opportunities.

Success and Failure on TV

Even the hardest work and the strongest desires don't guarantee that everything you do will be successful. It's natural that everyone experiences some failures at some point, even people like Jennifer Aniston. It's important that you keep working hard though. A few obstacles in the way of your goals shouldn't stop you from doing what you enjoy and working for what you want in life.

Jennifer sure didn't. After working in theater for a little while, she decided to move back to her hometown—Los Angeles. In Hollywood, she could easily audition for parts in TV shows and movies, since the film and television industry is based there. She tried out for and successfully got roles in several TV shows. They included a show called *Molloy* that aired for a very few episodes in 1990. After it was cancelled, Jennifer went on to star in a made-for-TV-movie titled *Camp Cucamonga*, a comedy about a summer camp where Jennifer played a relatively minor role. Her biggest role during this early period was in *Ferris Bueller*, a show based on the movie *Ferris Bueller's Day Off*. She played Ferris's sister for several episodes. But although the original 1986 movie had been wildly successful, the TV show was definitely not. She also acted in a short-lived comedy series called *The Edge*; each episode consisted of several skits and **parodies**. Finally, she was cast in another TV show called *Muddling Through* in 1994. She almost didn't audition for *Friends* because *Muddling Through* was nearly picked up for a second season. It was ultimately cancelled after its first season, and Jennifer was free to pursue other acting jobs.

That sounds like a lot of roles and a lot of work, but each series was quickly cancelled because of low ratings. But it wasn't Jennifer's fault the series were cancelled. A 1990 *New York Times* review praised her acting on *Molloy*, saying "Very nearly walking off with the show is *Molloy*'s older step-sister, Courtney, played . . . by Jennifer Aniston." She had raw acting talent, but she still needed a series to showcase it. Each time a show was cancelled, Jennifer was out of a job and had to start searching for another one.

Move to the Movies

Meanwhile, in the midst of trying out for a string of failed TV series, Jennifer turned to the movies for something different. Although she would later be very successful on the silver screen, Jennifer's start in the movie business was less than amazing. Her first movie was a 1992 film called *Leprechaun*. The movie was a mix between horror and fantasy, revolving around an evil leprechaun unleashed on a family. The critics hated it, and audiences stayed away. Combined with her failures on TV as well, this period was pretty frustrating for Jennifer, who almost considered

Jennifer's role on Ferris Bueller *might not have lasted long, but it was a big job for a young actress!*

giving up. Probably no one would have predicted that she would become a superstar in both TV and the movies!

She kept at it, though, and continued auditioning for roles. It was during this time that she learned about a new show open for auditions, called *Friends Like These.* That show would eventually be known simply as *Friends*, and it would launch Jennifer and the other leads on the show to stardom. Deciding to audition was one of the best decisions that Jennifer ever made.

CHAPTER 3

A SUPER-SUCCESSFUL CAREER

Words to Know

obscure: Something that is obscure isn't well known; not many people know about it.

negotiated: Negotiated means that people discussed something until they reached an agreement.

dominated: Dominated means that something stood out or got more attention than the rest.

paparazzi: The paparazzi are freelance photographers who chase after celebrities to take candid pictures for sale to magazines and newspapers.

tabloids: Tabloids are smaller illustrated newspapers that focus on juicy, sensational stories.

estranged: When people are estranged, they are no longer close.

evolve: To evolve means to continue to grow and change for the better.

F*riends* is perhaps one of the best-known TV shows of all time. Created and produced by David Crane and Marta Kauffman, it ran from 1994 to 2004 for ten seasons. It featured a cast of six friends in their twenties and thirties, who support each other through the ups and downs of life in New York City, including jobs, significant others, and having children. The apartment they share and the café called Central Perk that they frequent became well-known TV sets, and *Friends* sayings became part of everyday speech. Audiences often felt that these six people were their own friends.

It didn't take long for audiences to warm up to the new show; people were hooked on *Friends* right from the beginning. The show consistently received good ratings from both critics and audiences for all of its ten seasons. Both the concept and the characters rang true to those watching it. The success of *Friends* never faded, even though a lot of TV shows lose popularity in their later years. In the case of *Friends*, audiences stuck with it: over 50 million people watched the final episode on May 6, 2004, making it one of the most watched finales in sitcom history. The show's reruns are still frequently aired today, continuing to attract audiences. Some critics even believe that *Friends* is one of the best sitcoms ever created.

Before the Fame

But back before the first episode was ever filmed, there was no way of knowing how successful *Friends* would be. Five hundred actors auditioned in New York City and Los Angeles for the chance to play one of the main characters. The six actors who eventually landed the parts of Rachel, Joey, Ross, Monica, Phoebe, and Chandler took a chance on the new show. That chance turned out well for all of them, taking them from being

Few shows find as many devoted fans as Friends. *Jennifer owes a lot to her role as Rachel Green!*

obscure or unknown actors to household names. Jennifer Aniston was no different. In the end, she became perhaps even more famous than her co-stars.

When Jennifer heard about the show that would eventually be called *Friends*, she was originally supposed to audition for the role of Monica Gellar. However, she insisted on trying out for Rachel Green, believing that Rachel was better suited to her own character. She was right. Jennifer auditioned extremely well and got the part of Rachel soon after the audition. Courteney Cox Arquette landed the role of Monica. Once the other four characters were cast as well, the show was ready to start filming.

Building Up a Career

Friends went on to launch Jennifer Aniston to stardom. The five other cast members—Lisa Kudrow (Phoebe Buffet), Courteney Cox Arquette (Monica Geller), Matt LeBlanc (Joey Tribiani), Matthew Perry (Chandler Bing), and David Schwimmer (Ross Geller) all found enormous success as well. The cast worked together as a team, and no single actor or actress stood out as the main character. They **negotiated** salaries together, attended awards nights together, and became friends in real life as well as on stage. On screen, each actor received about the same airtime, and no one character's storyline **dominated** anyone else's.

For years, Friends fans wondered whether Ross and Rachel would get together.

Yet Jennifer seemed to gain a celebrity status that outshone them all. She stood out right from the beginning. Soon after the show started, people fell in love with Jennifer's . . . hair! Rachel's hairstyle on the show inspired millions of women to get their hair cut the same way. Dubbed "The Rachel," the layered, upturned hairstyle became a trend that reached women nationwide. While the hairstyle went out of fashion a few months later, it was the starting point of Jennifer's rise in people's affections.

Fortunately, hair wasn't the only reason that audiences loved Jennifer and her character Rachel. People wanted to see the spunky and sometimes spoiled Rachel figure out life. Rachel was a favorite character of many *Friends* fans throughout all ten seasons of the show. She is first a waitress at the Central Perk café, and later lands jobs at Bloomingdale's and Ralph Lauren. In season eight, she becomes a mother. By the end, the storyline concerning the romantic triangle between Rachel, Ross, and Joey attracted huge audiences during the last two seasons.

Along with the fame went a salary to match it. For the first season, each actor made about $22,000 per episode. By the last two seasons of *Friends*, Jennifer was making $1 million an episode. All six stars made that same amount, making them the highest-paid television actors in history. No actor has yet matched it, even a few years later.

International fame and a paycheck that large was a big step up from where Jennifer and the others had been before they auditioned for *Friends*. Jennifer's acting skills from school and her early Broadway and TV career had paid off. So had her determination and hard work.

A Highly Publicized Personal Life

As people became more interested in Jennifer, she had to learn to deal with more media attention. Fans weren't just interested in Jennifer's on-screen life; they also wanted to know every detail of her personal life. Celebrities, especially extremely popular celebrities, have to deal with *paparazzi* and *tabloids*. Their personal lives are under constant intense scrutiny from their fans. Jennifer's pictures appeared in gossip magazines, and people everywhere became interested in her every move.

At the height of *Friends*, Jennifer was frequently in the tabloids because of her relationship with equally famous actor Brad Pitt. Brad and Jennifer started dating in May 1998. They reputedly met on a blind date set up by their agents, and their relationship went on from there. They dated for two and a half years before marrying in July 2000. For a few years, they were the handsome Hollywood couple on every front-page news magazine. They seemed to be an example of a successful Hollywood marriage, a rare find in celebrity gossip.

But not everything was rosy during this time period. Although they stayed together for five years, Jennifer and Brad eventually split up. Divorcing is hard anyway, but it's especially hard when millions of people read about it on a daily basis. In a highly publicized breakup, Jennifer and Brad separated in January of 2005 and divorced a few months later in October. There was wild speculation that Brad had fallen in love with actress Angelina Jolie on the set of their film *Mr. and Mrs. Smith*. People even printed shirts

Jennifer's five-year marriage to actor Brad Pitt is still a big topic in the tabloids to this day!

that said "Team Aniston" and "Team Jolie," rooting for one woman or the other. When the couple finally got divorced, it made headline news. People couldn't get enough of the story, and the drama continued when Brad eventually dated and married Angelina.

Jennifer also revealed that she was **estranged** from her mother, Nancy Aniston. Nancy had given an unflattering interview to the press about her daughter a few years before, and had also published a book called *From Mother and Daughter to Friends: A Memoir*. Jennifer was upset at what her mother had said about her, and they had not been on speaking terms since. Jennifer

Thanks to Friends, *Jennifer seemed to be everywhere in the late 1990s and early 2000s!*

didn't even invite her to her wedding with Brad Pitt. However, Jennifer has since said that they made up after her divorce and are on the way toward healing their relationship.

Awards of All Sorts

Despite the ups and downs of her personal life, Jennifer earned lots of official recognition because of her acting skills as well as her off-screen personality. She was one of *People*'s "Most Intriguing People" of 1995, when she was just starting out on *Friends*. A few years later, in 2001, she was one of E!'s Top 20 Entertainers. Jennifer's style and beauty continued to captivate fans and critics as well. She was named as one of *People*'s Most Beautiful People in the World repeatedly in 1999, 2002, and 2004. In 2006, People listed her as the number-one Best Dressed celebrity in the world. People were fascinated with her, not just for her acting, but for her personality, looks, and charm as well.

Jennifer has also received many nominations for famous acting awards such as the Emmys, the Golden Globes, the Independent Spirit Award, the Screen Actors Guild (SAG) Award, the Kids' Choice Awards, and the Teen Choice Awards. Perhaps the most highly regarded prize in Hollywood is the Emmy Award. Her first nomination came in 2000, when she was nominated for Outstanding Supporting Actress in a Comedy Series for *Friends*. She was also nominated for the same category in 2001. Then, when she was nominated for Outstanding Lead Actress in a Comedy Series in 2002, she won! (See the beginning of this book for a description of the night.) She was again nominated in 2003 and 2004 but didn't capture another win. Her most recent Emmy nomination came in 2009, for Outstanding Guest Actress in a Comedy Series, for her appearance on the TV show *30 Rock*. Even though *Friends* might be over, Jennifer is still earning recognition for her acting.

Other awards recognized Jennifer's talent even earlier. The Screen Actors Guild (SAG) Awards is one of them. SAG is an American labor union that represents actors and others who work as performers in the entertainment industry. It nominated and awarded Jennifer, along with her five *Friends* co-stars, for the category of Outstanding Performance by an Ensemble in a Comedy Series in 1996. They were nominated again six more times from 1999 to 2004, spanning almost the entire run of Friends.

Other prominent awards Jennifer won include a 2003 Golden Globe, given out by the Hollywood Foreign Press, for Best Performance by an Actress in a Television Series, Musical, or Comedy, and a 2002 Hollywood Film Festival award for Hollywood Film Actress of the Year.

Jennifer received awards not just from professional critics but from regular audiences too. The People's Choice Awards is an award show where ordinary people vote from home. Jennifer has won more People's Choice Awards than any other prize. She won the People's Choice Award for Favorite Female Television Performer four years in a row, from 2001 to 2004. She was nominated four more times for various movies, and won once more in 2007. Clearly, TV and movie audiences have fallen in love with Jennifer Aniston!

After Friends

Even the most successful TV show has to end. *Friends* came to a close in 2004, after ten popular seasons. Some critics feared that the end of *Friends* meant the end of good sitcoms. It is true that no other sitcom has yet reached the same popularity.

And what would Jennifer do after the show that had helped her gain so much fame? Keep working, of course. Jennifer has said, "Isn't it funny? Your image of yourself is so different than other people's. I'm not good at hearing positive things—I can accept criticism better. I'm very critical of myself, which gives me some- thing to work on. I want to *evolve*." This is perhaps one of the reasons she's been so successful, despite skipping college: she continually wants to improve herself and her work. So naturally, when *Friends* had run its course and ended in 2004, rather than disappear from show biz, Jennifer moved on to more challenging work in movies and television.

CHAPTER 4
LIFE AFTER *FRIENDS*

Words to Know

typecast: If an actress is typecast, she is always picked to play the same kinds of roles.
acclaim: Acclaim is the praise and recognition someone receives.
grossing: Grossing refers to the total money earned.

Sometimes when a popular television series ends, its stars find it difficult to get other work. Sometimes, they need a rest. But this was not the case with Jennifer Aniston. She immediately went on to act in more movies. She also made guest appearances on other TV shows, and she started exploring other lines of work as well.

TV Life

Jennifer no longer appeared on struggling first-season shows. Now, she played characters on hit shows with excellent ratings. And she wasn't necessarily *typecast* as characters that were exactly like Rachel Green. For example, she guest starred on *30 Rock* as an old roommate who stalks one of the main characters. Her performance earned her a 2009 Emmy nomination for Guest Actress in a Comedy Series, her first (and so far, only) post-*Friends* Emmy nomination.

Jennifer has also appeared on the shows *Cougar Town* and *Dirt*. Both have ties to her good friend and co-star Courteney Cox Arquette, who starred in both. In *Dirt*, she plays a gossip magazine editor, and even shares an on-screen kiss with her friend. In *Cougar Town*, Jennifer plays an eccentric therapist. However, she hasn't yet starred as a regular in another sitcom. At least for now, Jennifer's professional life outside of *Friends* has mostly focused on movies.

The Movie Biz

Jennifer had clearly made her mark on TV, but she was ready to expand into movies too. Way before *Friends*, she had starred in the low-rated film *Leprechaun*, so she already had some experience with making films. However, since those early acting years, she's come a long way. Nowadays, she stars in commercial blockbusters that are immensely popular with movie audiences.

Even while starring in *Friends*, Jennifer dabbled in movie acting as well. She actually acted in several movies during the 1990s, but gained the most **acclaim** for her small role in *Office Space* in 1999, in which she plays a waitress with whom the main character falls in love. Then came her biggest box-office success: *Bruce Almighty*, which was shown in theaters in 2003. Jennifer played the girlfriend of the main character, who was played by Jim Carrey. This is the highest **grossing** movie starring Jennifer Aniston to date.

The new comedy from the co-writer of *Meet the Parents*

For the most cautious man on Earth,
life is about to get interesting.

Ben Stiller   Jennifer Aniston
Along Came Polly

JANUARY 16

In movies like Along Came Polly *and* Marley & Me, *Jennifer moved from working in television to being a star of the silver screen.*

In 2004 and 2005, she appeared in more box office successes, including *Along Came Polly* and *Rumor Has It*. In these movies, she had the opportunity to work with other big names in Hollywood, such as Ben Stiller, Phillip Seymour Hoffman, Alec Baldwin, Debra Messing, and Kevin Costner. Her name was just as famous as any of theirs.

Jennifer had clearly become a favorite in romantic comedies, and she went on to star in several more. In 2006, she appeared in the lead role in *The Breakup*. She received a lot of attention for

With movies like The Switch *Jennifer is continuing to make audiences around the world laugh.*

this role, but mostly because of her relationship with co-star Vince Vaughan. Many people know her best as the lead opposite Owen Wilson in 2008's *Marley and Me*. The film, which revolves around the life of a family dog, set the record for the highest Christmas Day box-office earnings ever, in part thanks to Jennifer's appeal.

Jennifer also has a history of starring in the lead roles of independent films, as opposed to the box-office hits that she's best known for. Examples include *The Good Girl*, in 2002, which received very good reviews from critics. The movie is a comedy-drama focusing on a department store worker (Jennifer) who has an affair with a man who thinks he's a literary character. She also starred in *Friends with Money*, which was shown at the Sundance Film Festival in 2006. It also received good reviews, although it was only released in a limited number of theaters in North America.

Her most recent films haven't done quite so well at the box office as in the past. In 2009, she starred in *Love Happens* with Aaron Eckhart, and in 2010, she was in *The Bounty Hunter* and *The Switch*. In 2011, Jennifer starred in *Just Go With It* and *Horrible Bosses* and in early 2012 she worked with Paul Rudd on the comedy *Wanderlust*. None of these movies received very strong reviews, and were not particularly successful in earnings. But Jennifer has proven before that she's a good actress, and she will undoubtedly do so again in the future.

Beyond Acting

With all her experience in TV and movies, it's no wonder that Jennifer wanted to try her hand at something different and get behind the camera rather than star in front of it. So besides act-ing, she has also dabbled a bit in film production and directing.

So far, she's founded two film production companies. In 2002, she created Plan B Entertainment with then-husband Brad Pitt and film producer Brad Gray. She eventually gave up her share in the ownership, leaving it to Brad Pitt. The company has a partnership with Paramount Pictures, Warner Brothers, and 20th Century Fox, and has released several big-name pictures such as *Charlie and the Chocolate Factory, Running with Scissors, The Time-Traveler's Wife,* and *Eat, Pray, Love.*

She must have enjoyed the experience, because she decided to start another company a few years later. Jennifer founded Echo Films in 2008. The company has a partnership with Universal Studios, and plans on producing several films that specifically star Jennifer. Another goal is to produce movies from meaningful books, and to portray human struggles and triumphs. So far, it has produced *The Switch,* one of Jennifer's movies in 2010.

Besides acting and producing, Jennifer has also worked on the directing side of things. In 2006, she directed the short film "Room 10." It starred well-known actors like Robin Wright Penn and Kris Kristofferson, focusing on the relationship between a nurse and an emergency-room patient. Apparently, Jennifer had wanted to direct for a long time, and this was her first chance. There had been talk of her directing an episode of *Friends,* but that had never panned out due to Jennifer's busy filming sched-ule. She's one of the only female directors out there, adding to the perspective that women can add to film production. She claims to have been inspired by Gwyneth Paltrow, another actress turned director who also worked on a short film.

Clearly, Jennifer is involved in all aspects of movie and film production. There's no telling what she'll do in the future; after all, she's only forty-one! She has many years ahead of her to continue to expand her career. Meanwhile, Jennifer has also turned her attention to other things besides her career, like charities and her personal life.

CHAPTER 5
JENNIFER TODAY

Words to Know

philanthropy: Philanthropy is work that does good for other people.
Down syndrome: Down syndrome is a condition with which some children are born. A problem with their genetic material causes them to have mental challenges. They will also be short and have flat faces.
autism: If a child has autism, he has a hard time interacting with others and his interests will be very limited. Some children with autism do not learn to speak.
humanitarian: Humanitarian has to do with activities that do good for human beings.
defamation: Defamation is false damage of a person's reputation.
tolerance: Tolerance is the practice or respecting others' beliefs and activities.
endorses: When someone endorses something, she gives her approval or support to it.

Jennifer Aniston has had a hugely successful career in TV and film. She's earned all sorts of awards, appears in blockbuster films, and has the freedom to try out different jobs in the entertainment industry. But there's more to her life than acting. She's branched out to a lot of other activities, both in the entertainment industry and outside it. She also spends her time doing things like charity work and enjoying her friends and family.

Doing Good with Success

A lot of movie and TV stars end up using their money and their time to do *philanthropy* work. Celebrities have lots of money to donate to charities, and they act as role models for others to follow their example. Over the past few decades, giving to charity has become an admirable trend among celebrities. Some pick one cause for which they publicly fight, while others act behind the scenes. Many celebrities even set up their own organizations to do work they think is important. Jennifer Aniston is no exception to this giving trend in Hollywood. She supports several different organizations that work to change the world for the better.

Jennifer has supported a long list of charities over the years. They include Friends of El Faro, a nonprofit organization that raises money for an orphanage in Mexico, along with the Lili Claire Foundation, which seeks to better the lives of children with *Down syndrome* and *autism*. Much of her charity work focuses on children: another organization she supports is St. Jude's Research Hospital, which is the third-largest health-care charity in the country, and which cares for ill children. The rights of women are also important to her. She supports RAINN (the Rape, Abuse, & Incest National Network), which works to end sexual assault.

For Jennifer, real success is about how you choose to help others.

Jennifer's support comes in lots of different forms. She has donated money to several of the organizations listed above, along with many others. For example, after the earthquake disaster in Haiti at the end of 2009, many actors donated their time and money to help victims. Jennifer herself donated half a million dollars to Doctors Without Borders, Partners in Health, and AmeriCares, all organizations working on offering relief to Haiti.

She has also donated her time and her enthusiasm to several organizations as well, despite her busy production schedule. Among her contributions include appearing in recent commercials for St. Jude's Hospital, along with hosting a movie screening to raise donations for AmeriCares, a relief aid and *humanitarian* organization. She and Courteney Cox Arquette have also headed a campaign in support of OmniPeace, a charity that seeks to fight for women's rights in the Democratic Republic of the Congo.

Much of her work also focuses on LGBTQ (Lesbian, Gay, Bisexual, Transgender, and Queer) rights issues. She has even received awards for her attention to this social issue. In 2007, GLAAD (Gay and Lesbian Alliance Against *Defamation*) decided that Jennifer deserved recognition for her work to promote LGBTQ rights. Every year, GLAAD nominates mainstream movies, TV, and actors for promoting *tolerance* and equality of LGBTQ individuals. In 2007, GLAAD decided that Jennifer's work on-screen had done a lot to familiarize audiences with

Few actresses have been as successful for as long as Jennifer Aniston!

LGBTQ lifestyles and points of view. The group gave Jennifer their Vanguard Award for her work toward this goal.

Appearances as Herself

Jennifer has become a famous name and a famous face, so there's a lot of demand to have her appear as herself on TV. She has spent some of her time advertising certain products. Companies know that audiences love her, and might pay attention if she *endorses* their product. She's probably best known for her appearance in Smart Water ads and commercials. Other companies for which she has advertised include L'Oreal (probably because of her earlier days when her hairstyle swept the nation), Microsoft, Heineken beer, and Damiani jewelry.

Jennifer also appears frequently on TV shows as herself. She has hosted *Saturday Night Live* a couple of times, once in 1999 and once in 2004. She has also presented prizes at awards ceremonies, rather than just receiving them. For example, she presented the award for the Best Screenplay at the 2004 West Independent Spirit Awards. Talk show appearances include *The Early Show*, *The Oprah Winfrey Show*, *Larry King Live*, *Late Night with Conan O'Brien*, *The Ellen DeGeneres Show*, *The Late Show with David Letterman*, and *The Tonight Show with Jay Leno*. That's a pretty long list; Jennifer is definitely in demand, since audiences are interested in hearing what she has to say.

Personal Life

Of course, Jennifer still has to take time to have a life outside of acting, producing, directing, and charity. Everyone has to have time to relax and to enjoy time with friends, family, and significant others. Jennifer remains friends with all of her cast mates from *Friends*. She is especially close to Courteney Cox Arquette. They reportedly visit each other frequently, and have stayed as close as they were while filming the TV show. Jennifer is even the godmother of Coco Riley Arquette, Courteney's daughter. She continues to work with Courteney, appearing in her newest TV shows and working together with her on charity projects.

As far as romance goes, Jennifer is very much in the news. Even though she is no longer married to Brad Pitt, people are still very interested in her romantic life. Millions of people eagerly read about her relationship and breakup with actor Vince Vaughn a few years ago. The pair began dating after co-starring in *The Breakup*, in which they played an on-screen couple. They became a real-life couple and dated for about a year in 2005 and 2006. They had to play down rumors that they were engaged and planning an $8 million wedding—and then they eventually broke up.

Jennifer's fans have most recently been intrigued by her reported romance with musician John Mayer. They have dated on and off since 2008, but recently broke up for good. Every move in the relationship, along with rumors about things that never happened, ended up in the press. Jennifer's relationship with actor Justin Theroux recieved a lot of attention from tabloids and celebrity magazines in 2011, too! Clearly, Jennifer's personal life is on display, whether she wants it to be or not.

Lasting Success

All of Jennifer's hard work has paid off—literally. After years of working in the television and film business, she's made quite a lot of money. She's also spent a lot of money! Her wedding to Brad Pitt in 2000 cost $1 million alone, while their house cost $13.5 million. In fact, Forbes rated her as one of the top-ten richest women in entertainment in 2007. She was estimated to be worth $110 million!

But Jennifer's success is more than just financial. She is a respected member of the Hollywood community as well, earning her praise from audiences, critics, and coworkers alike. Her numerous awards and recognitions prove it. Additionally, in 2007, she was invited to join the Oscar committee, also known as the Academy of Motion Picture Arts and Sciences. The committee is made up of almost 6,000 voting members, most of them actors. They vote to determine the Oscar winners for the year, an important highlight in the Hollywood year.

Jennifer has said, "I look at life like rock climbing. You get through the first tier, you rest for a minute, you look back and see how far you've come. Then you look up and you've got another tier to climb." That is certainly what she's done. From her first years acting Off-Broadway, to *Friends*, to her movie career today, Jennifer has gone through her ups-and-downs. But she has always continued working hard and striving for success. And she did it all without going to college.

Even though Jennifer never went to college, she has become a highly successful actress. But she still values a good education. She spoke about her work with children in a Mexican orphanage: "They have been given a lot of love and they're getting educated, which is the most important thing for them—to have an education and have knowledge of what they can do." That is exactly what Jennifer did with her own life—she got a good education at the start and knew what she could accomplish. Then she went out and did it.

WHAT CAN YOU EXPECT?

Of course not everyone who skips college is going to be a celebrity or a millionaire. But there are other more ordinary jobs out there for people who choose to go a different route from college. Here's what you can expect to make in 100 of the top-paying jobs available to someone who has only a high school diploma. (If you're not sure what any of the jobs are, look them up on the Internet to find out more about them.) Keep in mind that these are average salaries; a beginning worker will likely make much less, while someone with many more years of experience could make much more. Also, remember that wages for the same jobs vary somewhat in different parts of the country.

Position	Average Annual Salary
rotary drill operators (oil & gas)	$59,560
commercial divers	$58,060
railroad conductors & yardmasters	$54,900
chemical plant & system operators	$54,010
real estate sales agents	$53,100
subway & streetcar operators	$52,800
postal service clerks	$51,670
pile-driver operators	$51,410
railroad brake, signal & switch operators	$49,600

brickmasons & blockmasons	$49,250
postal service mail carriers	$48,940
gaming supervisors	$48,920
postal service mail sorters & processors	$48,260
gas compressor & gas pumping station operators	$47,860
roof bolters (mining)	$47,750
forest fire fighters	$47,270
private detectives & investigators	$47,130
tapers	$46,880
continuous mining machine operators	$46,680
rail car repairers	$46,430
shuttle car operators	$46,400
rail-track laying & maintenance equipment operators	$46,000
chemical equipment operators & tenders	$45,100
explosives workers (ordnance handling experts & blasters)	$45,030
makeup artists (theatrical & performance)	$45,010
sheet metal workers	$44,890
managers/supervisors of landscaping & groundskeeping workers	$44,080
loading machine operators (underground mining)	$43,970
rough carpenters	$43,640

derrick operators (oil & gas)	$43,590
flight attendants	$43,350
refractory materials repairers (except brickmasons)	$43,310
production, planning & expediting clerks	$43,260
mine cutting & channeling machine operators	$43,120
fabric & apparel patternmakers	$42,940
service unit operators (oil, gas, & mining)	$42,690
tile & marble setters	$42,450
paperhangers	$42,310
bridge & lock tenders	$41,630
hoist & winch operators	$41,620
carpet installers	$41,560
pump operators (except wellhead pumpers)	$41,490
terrazzo workers & finishers	$41,360
plasterers & stucco masons	$41,260
painters (transportation equipment)	$41,220
automotive body & related repairers	$41,020
hazardous materials removal workers	$40,270
bailiffs	$40,240
wellhead pumpers	$40,210
maintenance workers (machinery)	$39,570
truck drivers (heavy & tractor-trailer)	$39,260

floor layers (except carpet, wood & hard tiles)	$39,190
managers of retail sales workers	$39,130
cargo & freight agents	$38,940
metal-refining furnace operators & tenders	$38,830
excavating & loading machine and dragline operators	$38,540
separating, filtering, clarifying & still machine operators	$38,450
motorboat operators	$38,390
dredge operators	$38,330
lay-out workers (metal & plastic)	$38,240
forest fire inspectors & prevention specialists	$38,180
medical & clinical laboratory technicians	$37,860
tire builders	$37,830
dental laboratory technicians	$37,690
paving, surfacing & tamping equipment operators	$37,660
locksmiths & safe repairers	$37,550
sailors & marine oilers	$37,310
dispatchers (except police, fire & ambulance)	$37,310
pipelayers	$37,040
helpers (extraction workers)	$36,870

rolling machine setters, operators & tenders	$36,670
welders, cutters & welder fitters	$36,630
solderers & brazers	$36,630
gem & diamond workers	$36,620
police, fire & ambulance dispatchers	$36,470
models	$36,420
meter readers (utilities)	$36,400
mechanical door repairers	$36,270
public address system & other announcers	$36,130
rail yard engineers, dinkey operators & hostlers	$36,090
bus drivers (transit & intercity)	$35,990
insurance policy processing clerks	$35,740
insurance claims clerks	$35,740
computer-controlled machine tool operators (metal and plastic)	$35,570
license clerks	$35,570
court clerks	$35,570
fallers	$35,570
septic tank servicers & sewer pipe cleaners	$35,470
parking enforcement workers	$35,360
highway maintenance workers	$35,310
floor sanders & finishers	$35,140

tool grinders, filers, & sharpeners	$35,110
paper goods machine setters, operators & tenders	$35,040
printing machine operators	$35,030
inspectors, testers, sorters, samplers & weighers	$34,840
pourers & casters (metal)	$34,760
loan interviewers & clerks	$34,670
furnace, kiln, oven, drier & kettle operators & tenders	$34,410
recreational vehicle service technicians	$34,320
roustabouts (oil & gas)	$34,190

Source: Bureau of Labor Statistics, U.S. Department of Labor, 2008.

Find Out More

In Books

Aniston, Nancy. *From Mother and Daughter to Friends: A Memoir.* Amherst, N.Y.: Prometheus Books, 1999.

Johnson, Lauren. *Friends: The Official Trivia Guide.* New York: New American Library, 2004.

Marshall, Sarah. *Jennifer Aniston: The Biography of Hollywood's Sweetheart.* London, UK: John Blake Publishing, 2007.

On the Internet

Friends Fan Site
www.tv.com/friends/show/71/summary.html

High School of Music and Art
www.laguardiahs.org/about/history.html

Jennifer Aniston Center
www.anistoncenter.com

Jennifer Aniston Filmography
www.imdb.com/name/nm0000098

Jennifer Aniston Hairstyles
www.hair-styles.org/jennifer-aniston-hairstyles-picture-001.html

Jennifer Aniston Website
www.jenaniston.net

Index

Picture Credits

Angela George: p. 51
Brett Cove: p. 49
Chris Natt: p. 33
Featureflash / Dreamstime.com: p. 11
Fox: p. 22
Imagecollect / Dreamstime.com: p. 8
Miramax: p. 42
NBC: p. 18, 25, 29, 28, 30
sbukley / Dreamstime.com: p. 46, 34
Thomas Pintaric: p. 12
Twentieth-Century Fox: p. 38
Universal: p. 41

To the best knowledge of the publisher, all images not specifically credited are in the public domain. If any image has been inadvertently uncredited, please notify Harding House Publishing Services, 220 Front Street, Vestal, New York 13850, so that credit can be given in future printings.

About the Author

Kim Etingoff currently lives in Boston, Massachusetts. She grew up in New York State and graduated from the University of Rochester. She has since been pursuing her interests in sustainable farming, nutrition, and writing.